This is a story about your mother

This is a story about your mother

Louise Wallace

TE HERENGA WAKA
UNIVERSITY PRESS

Te Herenga Waka University Press
Victoria University of Wellington
PO Box 600 Wellington
teherengawakapress.co.nz

A catalogue record is available at the National Library
of New Zealand.

ISBN 9781776920716

Published with the support of a grant from

Printed in Singapore by Markono Print Media Pte Ltd

for Ethan

Contents

fact

i am breaking up with difficult poetry using   a comprehensive guide
to my biggest childhood crushes   then & now   thanks people

life is not a bed   of white paper   don't forget to stop and smell
a white piece of paper   by any other name

the tiled shower is not consented   the wall removals in the lounge
are not permitted   the vendor   is an A-grade arsehole   (fact)

murder podcasts   murder tv shows   '90s murder reenactments
on how our home appliances   will kill us all   in the new millennium

sometimes i forget what a proper noun is   (paris, not mata hari) survivor
is up to season 36 (ghost island)   and i will watch it as long as it's made

if i am ever stuck   in a frozen wasteland   for years on end
and have to walk out   i won't hesitate to cannibalise any real estate agents
they will be the first to go

ross   paul   keith   shane   other middle-class white-guy name

julie   ashlee   donna   jane   offer to come round for a cup of tea
when we're settled   to take my unborn baby for a walk   i won't
hesitate like i said

top 10 baby boy names   nz 2018   oliver   oliver   oliver   oliver
oliver   oliver   oliver   oliver   oliver   and oliver   now *that's* white

keep it together   no need to set yourself on fire   don't wear a tie
when using a blender   don't become a leader   don't make yourself a
target   don't use your immunity for anyone else

yesterday

my dad was angry   boiling   in his body how a kid gets   when they're
dog-   tired but tonight   I saw my dad really   laugh otherwise he's
absent   pacing grumbling unable   to be reached   the apologies   are
the worst first   he checks   no one is watching then mumbles   *sorry*
love   my father my child   the gentle person   we knew

/ / /

photos on the mantel   dad young sharp   and vibrant I used to love
finding cicada shells their thick   skins the best ones I'd keep   in old
matchboxes treasures   artefacts   but I don't *want*   an artefact
sometimes   life *is* terrible sometimes   there's nothing else to it
sometimes you watch   a game show at your parents' house   way too
loud   while your dad fades   into the couch sometimes you see   an
epic sunset like the whole sky   is on fire

/ / /

the   cicadas   are
trying   to consume my mind if the heat   doesn't get me first the fact
this sound is produced   by a special muscular structure repeated
contractions   and relaxations *that*   is going to consume my mind that
night   I dream of brains and ears   long needles   rapid punctures in
and out

/ / /

this place stinks   dad says as we enter the
building   for the support group and to say   otherwise   would
be lying I hold   his hand as we listen   to songs we shouldn't songs
about being half   a man songs about troubles   being far   away songs
I never   want to hear again his bedside   table is empty where   there
used to be a pile of books

/ / /

mum pulls   his belt on roughly dad
cries out   in frustration   this woman who   in this moment he can't
stand   but who he needs so desperately   he follows   her around
anxious   if she is out   of sight this man   who in this moment she

can't stand   who she showers cuts his meals   into pieces reminds him
what to do   with a fork but who   is the love   of her lifetime who was
who she met   at sixteen working   reception while he   was a radio
engineer charming   as all get out

                                    / / /

                                            the last trip   we took
together was a festival   when all we had to do   was be
cautious when   everything was not yet clear I watched   him at sessions
soaking   up words I had   to be on stage and was worried   about
arrangements a web   of arrangements I had made   and a backup plan
just in case *I'm sure   he's big enough to handle   himself* an organiser said
what the fuck   would you know I thought   *what the fucking fuck*   and I
thought   and thought it I'm still   thinking it but there's no one   I can
fight

        / / /

                        symptoms include   hallucinations *goodnight*   I say
to dad   and mean it almost everything   he has tried to
tell me this visit   he has been unable   to complete we separate   hesitate
just one more   hug   each more precious   than the last

                                                    / / /

we are beginning   our descent angling   closer to
earth and the plane's   hum shifts   to an overwhelming
drone flying   into nothingness   a numbness   there   I shelter from the
things that scare   me most I stroke   my belly   ballooning over the
seatbelt like a sunrise   I imagine saying   *let's pretend* as my dad   might
have once and so   we are beetles burrowing down   in the ground *this is
how   we'll survive* I say   to my son deep   inside   the sound

LIKE A HEART

aim for a healthy life

the first trying where it all begins trying all that trying even a trying trying ignore early trying trying and trying keep complex trying trying a trying trying and while the trying may seem to not be trying the trying you have started may have moved without trying trying your own trying and you never know exactly when trying although there is a small circle of trying trying generally for longer but only the most mobile of trying find their trying up trying into trying this trying and trying and trying of trying

it is still not time to get too excited

temperature rises
can lie in wait

for a German word translating
as middle pain

there is room
divide quickly

don't make plans and don't
sit around

in a field of sensitivity
be the dominant one

like a heart

forming channels / like a tube / like a heart / primitive / like a tadpole / like a nail head / like an orange seed / it is a chance / no greater than one percent / it is a personal decision / it is a risky time / for your relationship / you have a partner / who does not yet know / how the world works to whom / it is not yet obvious that / it has begun / you find yourself / confronting the news / and its effects / your disappointment / your delight / the guilt / of every woman / her worry / her joy / her excitement / her meltdowns / and it looks / as though you are lying / on your stomach? are you lying / on your stomach? / you may have a heavy sensation / feel more full / more physically ill / have you expected / you can do enough? / enough to prevent / someone else's body odour / the fumes of a car / of food / of perfume / your nostrils / are powerful are you feeling / lightheaded? / last week / is very similar to this week in how / you may be feeling / you worry / don't worry / you don't look / any different / it's a fairly classic / sensation / symptoms officially known / and counted by the calculators online / it's the best time / for your imagination / to wander when you haven't checked / that there isn't / something / going on

congratulations

you now contain ten
    little-finger-like projections you are being   extra careful you may be
    told   you are the only woman to ever swear and   you won't know
    it is a set-up you sense   you probably aren't responsible don't
    discount   a predetermined job

one hundred cells
    have now become ten   little-finger-like projections   of women
    swearing the effects   of women swearing   the process of women
    swearing discourage it   try   to give it up even   if it has been
    prescribed especially   for you

you report a sense
    of feeling   a protective wall   but you won't know   if it's a set-up
    you won't feel   it settling in   and dividing but you don't need   to
    go faster unless   it *is* a set-up   a predetermined   job you won't
    know   when it is settling   in

it is barely the size
    of a pin head   but it already knows where to go   and what   it
    has to do it doesn't   look anything like what   it will become but it
    knows   everything it knows centuries   beyond you

have confidence in fibre

come home to strip off your clothing. an outbreak of raising something from seed. say hello to an unwelcome second bout of adolescence. you still look like you might have friends. have confidence in fibre.

/

brush away unwelcome visitors. your own mum or other women who have had children but who are now officially hungry sex glands. be attentive to your toothbrush. to your own middle finger lifting up. try herbal tea or ginger beer or a blueberry the size of disbelief.

/

you wouldn't mind if they inherited your clothes but your youth is so far back. they may be sensitive to that family nose. those lips you get your power from. there is a thickening around your own abilities to speak of your excitement. brushing against the inside there is a little bean.

it's winter

sit facing the toilet which look
it's fine it's fact it's winter according
to the new seasonal fruit so shock
your life before it shocks you change
your partner change your wardrobe
your secret your small revelation
nurturing doubt hear the room hear
the strange thin levels that sound
a bit full in your mouth your vocals
their once serene chords like stone
tight like a budget ripe as the bulky
citrus fruit sharp and untrue

women's troubles

keepsakes & risky diaries, minor infections, siblings, roughage, fluids & cups,
scents & remedies, laundry cycle symbols, appointments, baths, gums, plans,
lists, sunblock, so & so, being bright, being nice, being tired, being certain,
being too efficient, too often, needing a wage, taking on work, taking up space,
protection versus control, allocation & influence, longing, waiting, returning
to public, standard maternal feelings.

night terrors

sneezing into yoghurt / moving with no sensation / money blowing away in the wind / custard / not moisturising / the navel in general / someone chewing almonds / someone shouting *TIME FOR A CUPPA?* / percentages / elevators / a problematic intake of cheese / a tickle in your heart / ridge in your brain / excess water in the body / total silence / noise / no contact or weak connection / no women / women / *whisper whisper whisper your subconscious is*

>> a deformed mother

> a creep with strange hair
> flooding

>> your mind
>>> pruning off

> common sense

>> you need company

and extra vegetables

> someone messages you about beans
> ice and other

superstitions

>>> not hearing

> when you say the word *coping* over

their frightening stories

>> that seem to grow
>> like lanugo

buy a small container they tell you

                    to store
            your many questions

better

to be organised
        than unattractive

                        nobody

          should find such great pleasure

   in muffins

blesséd goddess

keep this keep
a place
to sleep

just try
these items
your parents

won't shop
for alternatives
anyway

won't take you
on excursions
won't

correlate their
incredibly tempting
little urges urging

you at every minute
to brush
away your feelings

as if eating
was thinking
as if

cakes
were favours as if
inspiration

could happen from their
same
tired take

everyone's excuse
is to stay
head down

as if thinking
was unlimited
sipping water

along with
your favourite bands
a ginger-flavoured

something something
about smoking
move away

from your old
toxic group
don't patronise

me don't
pasteurise me
i am as timeless

as mysterious
as a rare
paté

crave

weak and irritable   the self flickers   time

is like a heaviness on your chest   you crave
but each moment   disappears

before you can hold it   you yearn
for night   to head off

into it   to occupy a bed   alone

cumbersome repetitions with friends

it's hard to be completely yourself while being beaten around the ears with leafy greens. you can see freedom swinging further away as you try to relax daily and not lift heavy things, blitzing vegetables and exposing your mood, poking out your chin and that no-good nose, your hair constantly increasing in volume so that everything feels like it might do you harm. oxygen seems dated. you don't mean to sound irritated, but can no one use an iron anymore? if you hear the phrase 'your little brain' one more time . . . and what does the term 'women's clothing' even mean when the designers seem to have totally forgotten your shape and the quantities of cereal you must now consume. there's no rest from judgement. you're keen to plan a holiday, a comfortable darkness, experience vague happiness and airline restrictions, frown at the food, lean your cheek in towards some regular and gentle insignificance.

some couples do a video

avoid risky behaviours   alcohol
and lost people

it's common   to hunger
for fruit   and fish alternately

even when you are reluctant   buy
the news   share the bathroom

salt apprehensively   bite
at pleasures

you are a constant production   tuned
to flora   a small bud   a small face

in the folds a little rump   a crown
and legs that will eventually bend

and be measured   still
in need of nails   and hair

officially   it can be a memento
some couples   do a video

ten to twenty
dollars   at the supermarket

you are now one   your cheeks
flutter   together when sleeping

when the world   comes bursting
to you   that's the right time

lucky x radiant x glow

black skirts and shirts x are meant
to be slimming x but the popular x taste
is to show off x your belly x the important
thing x is to go x against comfort x against
well-being x nature x is at capacity
and has been generous xx stop fretting
aka x multi-tasking x to try x is to suffer
and the work x isn't only in x the evenings
when x you have been blessed x with perfect
reflexes x and expenses x that lend
to bending xx mummy x they'll call you
which is lucky x when x you have no other
name xx everyone says x it will be hard x to say
goodbye x but you'll always remember x lying
looking x at the rest x of your body x the electric
sensation pulsing x from x your family x tree

the starring role

it's all about keeping up your outer. compression, not injections, and occasional treats. it involves a lot of smiling with straight teeth. what you might try is some Yves Saint Laurent. you're entitled to yoga products. it's a valid need to connect your skin to your brain to your eyes to your muscle. listen to your calcium specialist and halve your water retention. pasta is meant to expose a series of unrelenting levels, backwards tales that come quicker than headaches. it's these special diets that are the foundation of your old appeal, which you revel in losing often. think edible frenzy. think a dog gone gloriously rabid.

all you can hear in your dreams is barking

your legs make noises in bed. their little bones cooling through to loud gentle stretches. your whole life is visual waste, the numbness, the hopeless pursuit. you can't make a remedy from a clove. cookbooks won't provide a salve from disturbance. the cramps are a warning you should now be attuned to. what you're hoping for is a vivid door. a pathway leading away from the lives of dolly wives, dried stiff like hung garlic.

empty sex

the furniture is talking.
obviously.
have it out over the cooler months.
why the rush? you're breathless.
where's your stamina?
this should be rich and important.
a spicy, greasy act.
rediscover the quickening
in a brown ford.
support everyone's interests.
co-operate. be soothing.
ask. accommodate.
do your research.
keep up the chat.
what new wonders
can be found in undressing yourself?
or in skin responses?
the impact of mental extremes?
don't get despondent.
do your hair to get laid.
some say your little get-togethers
are a way of adding substance
where comparisons fall flat.
finally you feel proactive.
it's the ideal time
to plan an apocalypse-level
emergency foods supply
that can stay bacteria free.
put your energy and perspiration into this.

hot flex

MVP goes to your knees.
hardened, skinny, holding up

your large and powerful
quadriceps, your goddamn spine

these pins deserve
to be taken shopping.

/

sponsored ads for giant pillows
and aerobics can get fucked.

there is no space
in history for retail worries

when you look best in stirrup pants.
there is no weight but you.

/

gravity is so tiny
and you are so capable. how close time is

to your veins, your blood burning
up the atmosphere

until there's nothing left
but fumes.

take

care of cortisol take all offers of transport take a bra so big it has its own special challenges take anyone else's take and kick it into place take pace take a place in the movement of the queue it takes practice it takes nerve to be inside another life take every noise as a sign that it's all taking place it takes time it takes sleep it takes girlfriends and little gestures take connection take off to a restorative little world take hope in shying away take a voice that sounds generally thoughtful take peace in activity take insulation in household lives take repetitious time and chart each hour take as much quiet as the world can give until you can take your circulation and turn it into music

talk to your baby

this is the sound of waves / of no preference / of low-fuss mothering / or working
and staying reputable / the sound of being undercover / this is what it sounds
like to be secretly terrified / and this is the sound of washing / drying flatly / in
heat / the sound of a booster seat / being installed / this is the sound of intent /
of planning / and preparation / for something for which you can't prepare / this
is the sound of size / the sound / of a guarantee / and of hope / this is the sound
/ found / in a library / this is the sound of a screen / in the dark / the sound of
being online / this is the sound of temptation / fear / harm / hours / this / the
sound of uncertainty / of problems / change / the sound of being informed /
the sound of knowledge / and so also / the sound of support / and reassurance
/ but / there is further bad news / the sound of wilting posture / a continuous
slouch / the sound of breasts / and shoulders / ankles / the sound of mannerisms
/ walking / shoes / this is the sound of gravity / of stability / of the centre / of
earth / this is the sound of your advocate / of protection / of a shield / of comfort
/ the familiar / the sound of your body / and what's possible / here / the sound
of a shift / of adjustment / and this / the sound of seeing / what delight sounds
like / this is the sound of your voice / sounding off at the sound / fascination /
the sound of learning / of signals / the sound of so much potential / this is the
sound of light / and need / this is how it sounds to be tender / this is the sound
of your own skin

it may take years to declutter your bedroom

retentive agendas   dumping love   stories and studying folding   when the
bigger   picture is yourself   this emotional   hum   and your pleasure
in it. it's too early   for milk so you synchronise   to serene   a mere
component a bridge descending   in your own system.   you are anywhere.
you are in bed   visualising   moving. you delight   in your skills your
nervous   no-caffeine energy. days   whirl by until something   jolts and
you are back   with your mother her prompt   fragility in which there seemed
so much   empathy the realisation   your mother must have been emotionally
quite down   a pre-bed candidate   whose only interests shifted between
washing and paying for it   in anger. it's common   with your first and you're
asked   if you can empty   yourself and your vicinity   as though singing
should be by   timer as though   that's better   than being frustrated. that's
your women's   certificate your guarantee   that now you can raise   the
plumpest crop and somersault   away from any sadness   like a spark.

sexy springtime feelings

at twenty-five   you were special   born   for a social calendar
but now   you've got   a face made   for furniture and your right knee
is up against   the greatest challenge   of its life

/

you see   their active   sex life their choice   to only ever borrow
children   and unattractive thoughts   exude   as you stare biologically
and loathe   with energy   a shirt doesn't seem   to provide enough
insulation   from the noise

/

and so   a middle finger   towards awkwardness towards labour
of any kind   towards endless   obligation   let's start a cult
lack   of movement   with no   dynamic stretching   let's see
extended family at no more than bi-weekly   intervals let's   lift the lid
on good sleep and reawaken   sexy springtime feelings   let's avoid
deep   conversations after any   repainting wake   with no plan
let's   no longer limit   the amount of time
we spend curled   together

towards family light

swollen heels draining the irritation
from the rest of your body. your lungs

are unfurling. you are realigning
into a new model.

you are governing
and time soothes any sensitivity.

any old itches. storage
will sort itself out.

self-portrait

inward limbs stress
structures long
beautiful mechanisms

mirror, after showering

it's natural, rude and underlying, trying to take a very sweet but hard and scientific look at yourself, vigorously pondering your value, are you really really good enough, no no no you're lovely, your underlying is enlarging and you're valuing yourself, your lovely rude hair, a little pondering of small and of like, pondering your smalls, on and on and on, later or for so long and exclusively, there is a very sweet underlying enlarging, gaining on the rude and hairy little pondering, pondering on the small and on the less than natural, no no no it's like it's valuable or you're valuable after showering, trying to own the pondering on the safe and lovely you, enlarging yourself to lovely and enough to be rude and soft and unique and natural, no no no it's hard and scientific around an underlying and an enlarging, which is its own bright and very sweet scientific gain, it's unique and exclusive in the oily high elevation, pooling yourself to be rude and fresh and fresh enough, on and on and on around a new soft vigorousness, you are unique and valuable in the safe of yourself, you are lovely enough and so very very sweet and hairy and little, pondering on trying to be valuable after showering, a really really good value almost of your own, sucking the value into your own, exclusive and irritating, chewing its brightness and enlarging, lubricating, a vigorousness, less natural, hard and scientific, which is never enough and is irritating, chewing sweetness, a very sweet sweet high or a long unique newness all of your own, a hairy little unique version of yourself, vigorous and fresh, long underlying like your own enlarging with its own value or gaining on the very sweet sweet lubricating lubrication, the soft gaining on hairy, on and on and on, unique and after showering to oily to fresh, or with its own likeness like yourself so very sweet right through to oily, your own gaining on the trying, no no no trying, valuable in its safety and rude and hairy and little, and enlarging a rude and hairy little version of yourself, trying to keep yourself, yourself enlarging and underlying your uniqueness, you're less natural with no hard scientific underlying of your own likeness, gaining on the safety, enough to go later to a very sweet bright light, elevating and pooling and fresh and natural, no hard science, no little pondering, pondering on a rude and irritating chewing, its unique bright sweetness like a valuable softness with the safety of dreaming and smiling silently, a unique safety in the soft vigorous exclusivity of showering yourself and being lovely enough and pondering on small likenesses, almost all of it is like its own underlying self, rude and sweet and like its own long unique hairy little self, yourself a new really really good you, valuable and underlying and fresh, which is like pondering a really really good rudeness, high and sucking on an oily lesser self, it's really really good and natural with no hard science, no hard scientific science gaining on the safety of the really really good self, in and around the rude hairy little unique brightness, so that later on you're gaining on your own enlarging underbelly, the really really good and rude, pondering on yourself, so lovely and very very sweet after showering, lubricating your oily exclusivity, exclusive of yourself in showering, soft and after showering in the safety of your own uniqueness, which is underlying a fresh freshness, elevating a pooling of yourself, yourself in and of enough, a long longing of and in your own uniqueness, enough enough enough.

supply and demand

this is your one job
you are bound to and which elevates you
which is it?   you must balance your tendency
to hold on   to history   you must manage
your energy   cope
with heat
your midsection enough
to make
your shoulders
droop
                              you fall
as much as you can allow
your head your ears your back   a treasure
your bond   with your body running
into comments that see it   as an impairment
where family
is at the centre
                         it surrounds you
like a contract
like an unattractive attitude
its hands down   your top
                                   with a camera
now look now smile   take help
where you can get it or else
it will be gone fast

in time
you will see it's this host
body that bonds you
                        to other women
                        small
and tucked away as they may be
always saving   a kidney
or two   for someone else
please take it   honestly
i don't need it
it's yours

duty is a common concern

a nasty parasitic disease digging into your forehead. you feel a little fed up of swallowing and recycling to be honest. the benefits of your teeth seem to be fading. no matter what, excuse yourself from recording what you eat and from any boring book. you love a good photo album, and it's worth sharing that all anyone will remember of this is counting down to waking up.

relief

you have just made it
to the hardest

of the three weepy
floods

hibernation
as vengeance

breathe low
deep tears

the maternal bells are tolling

and trousers
no longer become you

friends sail by
with foreign offers

you used
to smoke in wardrobes

as a teen
now

you ache
with your new

little partner
pain

like a permanent
panic alarm

peak-feminine

while incubating you're ultra
peak peak-feminine

a shape so lovely so necessary
for us all. the process asks

for an indication of income
a vision of cash

too light
to rest on. the future

is a sneeze and in it
you practise holding

something heavy
inapposite to the advice

of the need
to drop everything.

medical

the endless bones
your belly   grimacing   calcifying
like a brick   you sigh   to the pit   right
to your floor

you are expecting   a stroller your own
careful breasts rising   what lies
under a bath   under lingerie   its sheer
developments

you are bad   at picking affairs and affairs
are measured by their differences   even fish
have plans   yours include
calisthenics

and marathon   toasting sessions
that fill   and consume you   in order
to ignore   the priorities
sucking

and tugging   wanting
and climbing you   leech-
like

medical department invocation

it's fascinating   how so many people are set   on increasing their muscles
when here you are   stationary   burning kilojoules   while sitting and
you won't stand   for this management   it gets worse   every   day
hospitalisation   is a footstool   an extendable chair and you've paid   for
the yellowish jelly so you're damn well   going to eat it you share   your
position   with strangers   and your resources seem fine   you can
kick   just as well as ever thanks   for asking people   are staring now
you are a storm   they gaze at   people are staring   at the amount
of books you own   that you have insisted   on bringing with you as
clumsy employment books   designed to lie or clear you   of lies with
their indentations   incantations   of thatched grief   you stash cans
you   can tolerate heartburn like no other   you are born   your bald toes
branching out   navigating   this new world

delaying tactics

in one sentence
how do you get a book deal?

if you removed as many responsibilities as possible
what kind of things would you write?

when people ask *what's your favourite movie*
what criteria do you use to narrow it down to just one?

on a scale of one to ten
how productive are you during episodes of insomnia?

how many times would you say
you need to test pool water?

how far into summer is too late
to start reading your holiday novel?

would you rather only be able to invite strangers
to dinner parties for the rest of your life

or have to listen to radio segments about protein
for an hour every day?

how can you get a very expensive ring back from a sibling
when you gave it to them as a gift?

after a chain of terrible dates
what happens to your breathing?

let's say you're curious
what's the ideal age to try stripping?

what options are there
for an elaborate wax job?

curriculum vitae

how clever, how clear you are
    having reabsorbed any possible final outcomes, you stretch your mind as
    far as a calendar, one you number yourself. you line a diary with sharp
    wet doubts, chronicling clothing and emergency linen as though some
    kind of insurance, until you wonder how other problems would feel,
    wrapped and packed like little disappointments.

your attributes include
    being physically bony like a rat, and the ability to handle the discomfort
    of being electrified. how can you ever be accustomed to love? or to cruise
    ship activities?

you catastrophise
    imagine profuse cracking of ribs. you protest your own health, add more
    angst, get more hormonal. you cover your food in carribean coating, as
    though a signal for coping.

you jinx yourself
    by recording dates, making bookings like it's a fear, like you're keeping
    people waiting. this nagging energy is normal. visualise a nature setting
    and just pivot.

cleanup

in the black, back parts of your mind are big achy lists padded with housework. the outline of stains and subconscious pressure. the complex mothers resist this. they separate it out using their hard jaded eyes. the only nests are in their mouths.

/

options are offered as if there's a choice, but even these will soon disappear. there is a genuine tinge before your selves separate. each hour becomes fused to the next. you may look calm, but that's just a sign of infancy.

/

when it comes you imagine a frenzied sticky shift, having to suck it up atop a sheet, getting it all out in clumsy positions. but honestly, don't fret, chores simply delay decay. no one cares how long you mop the bathroom for. a watery storm is on its way.

pep talk for a sap

fuck your early education about bras, you've done your difficulties. it's time to get your veins to work. nurture yourself into a normal state. your body is refocusing, it's a test. liquor simply leaves the burden to someone else. plus it's not allowed, dummy. you are just a common baby, about to be thrown into the fire, bigtime. it's about taking your heart with you, taking a rolling break, holidays aren't a thing you'll experience anymore. your head hasn't grown on any significant scale, stop panicking. a pelvis needs to be taken seriously, and you're never going to feel like you know what you are doing. most days end with doubts gushing from your nose. all of your reason is now held in your nipples. and inaccessible. if you had any interest in law, you would have demonstrated that by now. you won't be expanding your education in classes over summer, forget it. instead you're gnawing as though contagious. and that's fine. no one's watching, even if you'd like to think they are. why don't you focus on how you want to be with the ones you truly love? right now, you're unnaturally quiet. you are mentally counting your no-employment. it's forever by the way. verses won't help. for fuck's sake, use this time for good! appeal for the use of less plastic. rewire the world against the rich. there's no time to be courteous in your state. get immoral. reflect on some genuine questions for once. *can somebody please find my youth?* no, because it's gone. so get on with it.

kickoff

you've come   without your senses you suddenly sense   you'll be sick
so you come into a strong   standing position an attempt   to override
it and you see your shape's reflection   full   of positivity and volume
your full body   its power do not   turn away come   to a room
that will serve   to conserve you familiarise yourself   with difficulty
how difficult   you can be to care for how difficult   *can* you be
to care for? so care   for your providers at least remember   their names
remember every time you felt   too overwhelmed to trust   and forget it

total recall

the health professionals are discussing
    the length of your wall   how thin   how much longer   to wait
    how to move   an event   an artificial wonder   you are restless
    but strong they wonder   are you ready   for reprieve? ready   to show
    your loyalty   to faith and sex?

the health professionals are discussing
    how life hinges   on pain how distractions   are important like
    thai cookery   and painting how it's   as simple as an apple
    ripening   you are less unique   than you think just think   of it
    as owning   your truth write that   on a post-it   you've only been
    crying   because you're mentally   overdue but life   hinges on pain
    hinges   on the big jobs   which will always weigh   significantly
    you're essentially tired   they say but it's all over   to you this new
    life   ahead hinging on your attitude and ultimately   thai cuisine
    is not going   to cook   away the days

the health professionals are discussing
    how they will use   a series of strong   little scares how these past
    fears   carry you how walking   might be difficult   how you
    might feel strange   within yourself like being small   in a big house
    and now they are discussing how you'll feel   just before you wake
    but you've been awake   all this time in the darkest   room   *stay*
    calm   you hear them say as your limbs   begin to snake your body
    waking into being   something entirely new   building   yourself
    slowly up   and out of that place

you're quite good at everything

you once fitted
into an unwanted purple Versace

you love a good chart
you have the ability

for sudden fierceness
and you plan to breathe

to the point
of sickness

to kick yourself
towards engagement

slinging your emotions to the corner
in a bucket

until there's a scramble inside, a frenzy
of impatience

relief will come
as a gush

you'll experience a new and phenomenal relationship
with your vagina

the little evictee ringing and truly needing
in its opening minutes

feeding
as if immune

to your accomplishment
while you drink down

a mixture called gingerly
or tenterhooks

and you stand
holding yourself

in that first
shower

small and reassuring interactions with your mother

you're done baby now you can just be way more contracted everyone will have very approximate general reassurances to extend their supportive faces asking if you'd like a bath if you'd like to soft-out in a watery mass would you like to come to the simplest life? would you like to become some sort of rare and translucent chemical infusion?

/

the advice to new women is to shield yourself from interaction the infection is the role of the home welcoming it into your skin you are keen for some social reality you'd be willing to give massages to hundreds of different people just to accumulate touch like a tsunami

/

everyone is looking for why everyone is seeking a beginning all these demands from people you have to try to shut out because what you're experiencing is some kind of emotional hearing and what you've longed for is to feel things and now you feel so many

/

sweetness is commonly the last thing wanted just a waste product your body overcompensating in the region of your nails until you have to frequently towel your fingertips off for blood but keep congratulating yourself honey you're doing a great job

VESSEL

This is a story about your mother.

There are some things you cannot know.
There are some places I cannot go.

Here is the shape of one.

                    (A cane basket).

Here
           is the shape of another.

    (An unfinished hull).

My father tried to build a boat he never finished.
I see it everywhere.
The boat can hardly hold

      its burden.

             How well

   he would have loved you.

People are phoning every day to ask if there's any news. I drink raspberry leaf tea. I walk around the neighbourhood with one foot on the road, the other raised on the kerb. It looks as stupid as it sounds. I keep a list of names on a small whiteboard. Friends say I shouldn't get so hung up on their meanings. But *Carson* means swamp-dweller and *Calvin* means bald.

This is a story about your mother.
Just like every other story.

Birth is unpredictable. Despite medical advancements, the risk of death for mother and/or infant remains. We spend a whole session at antenatal class on incisions and interventions. I have a machine that will give me small electric shocks at the base of my spine when it is time.

People are talking about nesting and getting things *ready for baby*. I am trying to finish an article on literary journals. I doubt I will be a good mother. I might be a terrible one.

Try to picture me.
Try to imagine my face.
I wonder if you will think of me

      when I no longer know

                    I'm here.

  In sailing,
you must learn how to demast:

           how to cut away

   the mess.

There are many different scales of pain.
Some are songs.

                    Some linen

          with white lace trim.

How small they seem, you'll say,
      when you hold the clothes

    I once thought hard about for you.

                In an instant,

      we transform.

I phone the midwife and beg her to come. We are still not at the required length and frequency of contractions, but she says she can *hear it in my voice*. I hang up and am sick all over the bed. She arrives and says we have to go to the hospital. *Now.* I tell her that I don't think I can make it and I'm scared to try. *That's okay*, the midwife says, *we can deliver the baby here*. I wanted gas. I wanted the option of an epidural. I wanted to try the pool. But birth is the body's intuitive process: it doesn't care what we don't know.

The ambulance comes to wait at the house, in case of any *complications*. The officers lean on our dining table as though waiting on a coffee order. *You can have a seat*, I keep offering, on all fours. Can't they wait in the van? *We're fine*, they say, pleasantly. I grit my teeth and bear down.

The midwife calls it after two unsuccessful hours. We need to go to the hospital. As we leave the house, I am worried about the lights being left on. The officers strap me to the gurney. I look out at the darkness through the ambulance windows, and feel the sway of the vehicle as we wind around the bays.

Birth is the body's intuitive process.
And people walk tightropes all the time.

There is now a whole fleet

of waiting vessels.
                              An envoy

        at the edges of my eyes.

At the hospital the delivery feels brief, but I find out later it was another couple of hours. They use the ventouse: a small suction cup that attaches to the baby's head to try to pull him through the channel. It seems to work but as soon as the cup is removed, I feel my baby slide back up. I wail. His heartbeat starts to drop. It's never good to see health professionals looking worried. The midwife calls for the doctor who rushes in and reattaches the ventouse. They yank the baby out, like a couch through a doorway. I feel a biblical gush. Birth is unpredictable and we are relieved and tearful to see our son.

In the days following, I am weepy. We do a lot of lying down and holding. There are things I don't want to think about. There are things I don't want to imagine. In the weeks following the days, I push the pram around the neighbourhood. Orange marigolds observe me walking past. I sit on the driveway, my baby nestled in my arms. I draw squares on the concrete with coloured chalk. One inside the other, inside the other.

They say this is easy: *the most natural thing in the world.* When I am alone in the bathroom, I don't always want to come out. I push my body against the cool tiled walls. I hear screaming in the depths beyond the door. I wake sweating in the night, urgently searching through the bedsheets. But he is asleep in the bassinette beside me. He is bundled safely, ready to be nudged from a riverbank, to bob along in search of a better mother. He is asleep in the bassinette beside me. He is beside me.

Try to picture me.

                    Sunlight beams

through the window
but I do not yet feel myself.

It shines
            on blue pathways that run under

your skin,
            passages filled
                        with life.

                 You smile and I feel

            your forehead on mine.

As well as pain,

               there is joy.

Think of something you know about me.
Something you know for sure.
Step on it with both feet.
Make sure it can hold your weight in water.
Make sure it can hold you a long time.

We knew who you were as soon as we saw you.
The second they pulled you from my body.
The name means firm or strong, and you are beautiful.

Other names mean

                              courageous.

              Voyager.

In some other place, you finish building
                    the boat my father no longer can.

        Some lines can't be cut.

                        I know

        how to move now, I know
                        how to breathe.

Swaddle the hull's ribcage in wooden sheets.
I am ready to sail with you.

Notes

The title 'fact' refers to the Craig Dworkin poem of the same name: an exact list of ingredients that make up a (white) sheet of paper but also a changing poem, where each time he releases it, he alters the list according to the make-up of the medium it is being displayed on.

The title 'yesterday' and various references in the poem refer to the Beatles song. The line 'sometimes life is terrible' is a riff on the line 'life sometimes is horrible' from Arthur W. Frank's text *The Wounded Storyteller: Body, Illness and Ethics.*

The poems in the sequence 'like a heart' were constructed using text lifted from the Huggies' week-by-week pregnancy guide and fed through Gregory Kan's *glass leaves* manipulation app (for which I am grateful), then edited and shaped into their final form. Added to. Edited. And edited again.

Acknowledgements

It takes a village – babies and books / / / Rory and Ethan, for holding tight with me on this unimaginable journey, providing smiles and laughter through wild weather; thank you for being what matters most / / / The Aotearoa writing community (colleagues, friends, whānau), especially all those who read portions of this, provided feedback and supported the collection, thank you: Francis Cooke, Chris Tse, Gem Wilder, Lynley Edmeades, Jacob Edmond, Emma Neale, Vincent O'Sullivan, Sarah Jane Barnett, Fergus Barrowman, Ashleigh Young, Anna Knox, Te Herenga Waka University Press and Ebony Lamb / / / Journals and festivals that made space for this work: Dunedin Writers and Readers Festival & Claire Finlayson, *Ghost City Review* & Justin Karcher and John Compton, *Landfall* & Lynley, *min-a-rets* & Sarah, *NZ Poetry Shelf* & Paula Green, *Peach Mag* & team, *The Spinoff* & Chris, *Sport* & Fergus, Ashleigh, Kirsten McDougall and Craig Gamble, *takahē* & Erik Kennedy, Verb Wellington Readers and Writers Festival & Claire Mabey and Rijula Das / / / Anna Perry, for your creative friendship and collaboration and use of the beautiful cover image / / / For mothers of all kinds and those who have wished to be / / / Thank you to those who supported us as new parents, who lifted me and who continue to be a source of love in Ethan's life: Amanda & Dan, Cathie, my extended Matthews whānau, Pam & Doug and Ruth, Natalie & Richard and for Fernando, Sophie & Gracie, Anna & Maxwell, Rieke & Jonas, Kirsty, Meseret, Michelle, Victoria & The Book Club, Lynley & Neil and Molloy, Emma & Matt and Naia, Amy & Nigel and Ollie & Lucas, the Otago University English & Linguistics Department, and staff at Te Maioha & Te Puna of the Otago University Childcare Association / / / I think I am forgetting a lot of people and can no longer blame that on baby-brain / / / Thank you to my own mum (and sorry about all the swearing), who always told me I was doing a great job: the best thing you can say to a new mother / / / And for my dad, who I have loved and will love, forever.